ONE MONTH TO A MORE LIFE-GIVING RELATIONSHIP

31

WAYS TO SHOW HIM WHAT LOVE IS

WAYS TO SHOW HIM WHAT LOVE IS

One Month to a More
Life-giving Relationship

Alyssa Bethke

NELSON
BOOKS

An Imprint of Thomas Nelson

Published in Nashville, Tennessee, by Nelson Books, an imprint of Thomas Nelson. Nelson Books and Thomas Nelson are registered trademarks of HarperCollins Christian Publishing, Inc.

Published in association with Yates & Yates, www.yates2.com.

Thomas Nelson titles may be purchased in bulk for educational, business, fundraising, or sales promotional use. For information, please e-mail SpecialMarkets@ThomasNelson.com.

Any internet addresses, phone numbers, or company or product information printed in this book are offered as a resource and are not intended in any way to be or to imply an endorsement by Thomas Nelson, nor does Thomas Nelson vouch for the existence, content, or services of these sites, phone numbers, companies, or products beyond the life of this book.

Scripture quotations are taken from the ESV® Bible (The Holy Bible, English Standard Version®), copyright © 2001 by Crossway, a publishing ministry of Good News Publishers. Used by permission. All rights reserved.

ISBN 978-1-4002-2871-3 (eBook)
ISBN 978-1-4002-2865-2 (TP)

Library of Congress Control Number: 2021944974

Printed in the United States of America
22 23 24 25 26 LSC 10 9 8 7 6 5 4 3 2 1

CONTENTS

NOTE TO READERS

F irst off, you rock. By buying this book and going through it with your significant other, you obviously are already dominating at life! Jeff and I have prayed over this project and really believe it can be a fun way to cultivate a healthy relationship and bring back the joy and intimacy that sometimes gets lost amid the everyday activities.

To get the most out of this book, we'd first say *lean in*. Lean into the ideas, the spontaneity, and the parts that stretch you the most. Don't be afraid to just go for it. Have fun and create memories. These books were a collaborative effort, and we are firm believers that with this book (written from Alyssa's perspective), as well as with *31 Ways to Show Her What Love Is* (written from Jeff's perspective), whatever you put into it you will get out of it. Isn't that true with all our relationships as a whole? Also know that this is just a template. Some things won't be a good fit for your relationship or aren't doable based on certain locations, resources, and other variables.

We have tried to make every day as applicable for everyone as possible. With that being said, feel free to morph it, change it, adapt it—do whatever you need to do to get the most out of it. The goal isn't to rigidly follow this book and "cross each day off your checklist," but rather it's to bring a fresh vibrancy and life back into your relationship.

Also, a quick additional note to the dating folks out there. Obviously we are married, so we are coming from that perspective. But we also wanted to write this as a useful tool for dating couples. You might have to change it up in a different way. When not living together, some of these are a little harder to manage. Since you're dating, you probably don't see each other every day. So feel free to stretch this out over a few months or pick just a few to do each week.

We're rooting for you!

SUPPORT HIM
WITH PRAYER

———

To this end we always pray for
you, that our God may make you
worthy of his calling and may fulfill
every resolve for good and every
work of faith by his power.

—2 THESSALONIANS 1:11

Hands down, the best thing you can do for your man is pray for him. I'm often tempted to do something else, something "better" or more noticeable. And doing other things is great and totally part of pursuing him—hence this book! But prayer needs to be the foundation. I can't tell you how many times I've prayed for Jeff and then have been amazed at how God has moved in his heart. But even more important, I think prayer is what moves my heart to love and pursue him. I've found that when I'm consistently praying for Jeff, I'm way more patient, kind, and gentle with him; I find myself cheering him on, being intentional, and putting him first.

A lot of times, too, I don't know the best way to pursue Jeff. What could I do to show him I love him? That I'm thinking of him today? Lately, when I've asked the Lord to show me how to serve and love Jeff, He leads me to do something that ends up totally blessing Jeff that day. God knows our men the best, so why don't we ask Him to show us how to love them?

I admit that I'm not consistent with praying for Jeff, but I so long to grow in this area because when I do, it rocks! Some of the lies that we can entertain about prayer are that it's too easy, it won't do anything, and we can do things better than God. Or sometimes we're just lazy. But the Lord loves it when we talk to Him. Prayer doesn't need to be perfect, planned out, or sound "spiritual." It just has to be real. You can talk to God about what you're hoping for your man, areas you'd love to see him grow in, questions you have, or it can be powerful to pray verses over him. (I'll suggest some verses today to get you started.)

LOVE IN ACTION

Let's begin this journey with uplifting your man before your heavenly Father who is the One who knows and loves him the best.

- Ephesians 6:10–20: Pray that he'd put on the armor of God, being well suited for the spiritual battles that he faces each day.
- Psalm 24:4: Pray that he'd be pure in heart, clinging to what is good and hating what is evil. Pray that he'd fight against any temptation to entertain lustful thoughts.
- Pray that he'd have wisdom as he goes about his day today, making decisions.

YOUR THOUGHTS

_____

_____

_____

_____

_____

_____

_____

_____

_____

_____

_____

_____

_____

_____

_____

_____

_____

_____

_____

_____

_____

CHOOSE A SCRIPTURE

---

*Your word is a lamp to my feet
and a light to my path.*

—PSALM 119:105

S cripture is full of prayers and songs of praise! Throughout the Old Testament we see men and women talking to God and giving Him praise for all that He's done. Then, in the New Testament, we read letters written by the apostles that include prayers they're praying for believers in certain towns and cities. Many times, those same prayers have been my prayers for my family, friends, and myself. I love praying through certain verses, because as I do so, it draws me closer to knowing who the Lord is as well as gives me wisdom in how to pray for those I love. Because sometimes I just don't know what to pray for.

LOVE IN ACTION

- Going along with yesterday's call to action, today I'd like you to choose a verse to memorize and pray over your man for this next month. Maybe it's a verse you've been reading lately, or something that the Lord lays on your heart.
- Write out the verse and frame it.
- Give it to your man, telling him you're praying this verse over him this month. Even if he doesn't know how to respond to this gesture, or doesn't say much, I know it'll really touch his heart to know you're praying for him.

YOUR THOUGHTS

DAY 3

MASSAGE HIS FEET

———

Serve one another in love.

—GALATIANS 5:13

Jeff's all-time favorite thing is getting his feet massaged. If there is one way I can serve him, it's that. If we're debating over something and we decide to bet on it, if I throw out that I'll massage his feet if I lose, he's all in! If I don't know what to get him for Christmas or his birthday, I always have lotion and a foot massage to lean back on. It's just the best in his book.

And if I'm totally honest with you, I have to talk myself into doing it every time because, *gross*. I mean, I adore my husband, but touching his feet isn't on my list of favorite things to do. Seeing how much Jeff loves it, however, gives me joy. I love being able to serve him in this way, a way that I know really blesses him. It helps him relax and shows him that I'm thinking of him and am paying attention to his favorite things.

LOVE IN ACTION

- Today, give your man a foot massage (or back massage if he likes that better).
- It doesn't have to be a sixty-minute, five-star-spa massage! Even just five minutes shows him that you are thankful for him and thinking of him.

YOUR THOUGHTS

MAKE HIS FAVORITE SNACK

———

Love is kind.

—1 CORINTHIANS 13:4

The other day Jeff was taking a nap, but I knew he'd be getting up soon and would need a little snack because dinner was still a ways off. I looked in our fridge and there were celery sticks already cut up. So I decided to just throw together some ants on a log (celery with peanut butter and raisins). Okay, I didn't "just throw them together." They're actually a little more time-consuming than I realized! Thanks, Mom, for all those hours you spent making them for me while I was growing up!

When Jeff woke up, he was a little cranky. I'm just being real with ya'll here. I mean, let's be honest, sometimes you wake up from a nap feeling like you just won the lottery. And other times you feel worse than before you fell asleep. This was the latter for my man that day. But when he saw the ants on a log on the kitchen counter waiting for him, his face lit up and his entire demeanor changed. He ate those bad boys and was a whole new man.

LOVE IN ACTION

- Today, prepare your man's favorite snack.
- If he loves _____ (pistachios, blue corn chips, etc.), buy a bag for him!
- Or it can be something super simple to prepare like cut-up apple slices or microwavable popcorn. Just think of something that he likes and have it ready when you see him today.

YOUR THOUGHTS

DAY 5

PLAN A SPECIAL
DINNER

—

Whoever said, "Food is the way to a man's heart," hit it right on the head! No truer words have been spoken when it comes to my husband. He loves eating and he loves food, *good* food. (I mean, who am I kidding? *So do I*!) If you come to our house for dinner and we are eating something that Jeff loves, he'll give me a standing ovation and bang his hands on the table (sure makes a girl feel good). Kinsley, our oldest daughter, does the same thing now when she likes something. It's too cute!

I'm guessing that your man likes food too. And even if he isn't a true foodie, I'm pretty sure he appreciates a good meal provided for him. This week, plan to make him a dinner you know he really enjoys. For some of you, this totally excites you! You love to cook. You're pulling out your Pioneer Woman recipe books or scrolling through Pinterest to find the perfect meal. Or you may be wanting to ignore this because cooking is just not something you enjoy. So I'm just going to say this: *grace and freedom on you*! If you love to cook, then you go girl! You get at it! But if it's not your thing, that's okay.

LOVE IN ACTION

- If you love to cook: plan, prepare, and surprise him with his favorite meal.
- If cooking isn't your thing or you have a time challenge: Make something really simple that you know he likes, or grab take-out from one of his favorite restaurants. There's nothing to prove to him or yourself. What's important is showing him you care by providing a good meal you know he likes. (And if that good meal is a Happy Meal from McDonald's because that's what he likes, then awesome!)

YOUR THOUGHTS

PRAY FOR
YOUR MAN

———

Pray without ceasing.

—I THESSALONIANS 5:17

O n Day 1, I offered my thoughts on the importance of prayer. I want again to stress its value. I'm longing to grow in praying for Jeff more consistently. When he's traveling, I find myself praying for him much more often, probably because we don't talk nearly as much as when he's home. So I take his heart to the Lord instead of relying on myself to love him. But when we're home together, I often forget to pray for him because I'm talking to him all the time and I think I just take him, or rather the fact that I'm with him all the time, for granted. It's easy for me to pray for everything else, like my kids, my worries or friends, and neglect praying for him.

But on top of just longing to pray for him more, I also want to grow in praying over him; when he's right there beside me, to put my hand on him and lift him up to the Father. Sometimes when Jeff's struggling with something, he'll come to me and ask me to pray for him. And every time, it's like I'm caught off guard. Like I forget that's something God calls us to do. Every time I do pray for him, it's so beautiful. Jeff is totally vulnerable with me, humble to ask for help, and I get to join with him, going to the Father with his concerns. What an honor!

It may feel awkward at first to pray for your man or you may be embarrassed or shy. But don't be! It is a huge privilege and one that will not only bless him but also bring you closer as you go before the Father together.

LOVE IN ACTION

— Today, ask your man if you can pray over him. It could be before he goes to work, before bed tonight, or in the middle of the day.
— Thank the Lord for this man of yours and pray for his heart and mind, for his work, protection, and purity.

YOUR THOUGHTS

ENTER HIS WORLD

—

P art of loving your man is doing what he loves to do—entering his world. For example, one way I show my daughter Kinsley that I love her is by intentionally playing with her. So, you may find me on all fours, crawling around our coffee table, chasing her. Or, I may put on her princess crown and sit crisscross on the floor with all her stuffed animals surrounding us as I read a book to her. Not only does she love it, but I love it because I get to be a kid again and just love being with my little girl.

Guys are the same! One way they bond with another person is by sharing an activity. Jeff can go hiking, paddleboarding, or shoot some hoops with another guy and automatically they're connected in some way. In relationships, I think it can be easy (especially in marriage) to get into the habit of doing your "own thing." Find an activity he likes that you can share.

LOVE IN ACTION

Think of one thing that your man loves to do. It may be a sport, a certain genre of movie, a book that he's currently reading, working out, cooking, gardening, music, cars, and so on. Today (or sometime this week) do that hobby with him. Here are a few specific suggestions:

- Watch that movie with him that he's been dying to see.
- Watch his softball game and cheer him on.
- Pick up a copy of the book he's reading and read it together.
- Listen to him play guitar.
- Ask him to show you something about cars.

Enter his world this week.

YOUR THOUGHTS

PROVIDE A
BREAKFAST TREAT

———

About six months into dating Jeff, he got a new job and had to travel a lot. I mean a *lot*. Like every week. Some trips he would land in Seattle at two o'clock in the afternoon and have to fly back out at five o'clock that same night. To say it was hard for me is an understatement! I mean, I loved that he was loving what he was doing and was so filled up, but man, I missed my guy.

For one of his trips, I got to drive him to the airport early in the morning because I didn't have work that day. I hadn't seen him much, so we decided we'd stop for a quick coffee date before he flew out. Obviously we could order coffee (mmmm, coffee) and pastries, but I wanted to make it a personalized little coffee break for us, so I whipped up some cream cheese peach muffins

1. because he loves cream cheese,
2. because he loves anything peach, and
3. because I straight up love muffins.

23

I put them in a basket with pretty napkins and a note and brought them into the coffee shop with us.

A muffin is just a snack to Jeff. He needs the full meal deal: eggs, potatoes, toast. Regardless, he loved those muffins, but I think he loved even more that I thought about what he likes and made something special just for him. And really, it didn't take that much of an effort on my part.

LOVE IN ACTION

- Today, think of a fun breakfast treat that your man would enjoy (muffins, cinnamon rolls, donuts, bagels, and so forth).
- Meet up with him tomorrow morning and share your treat together. If that's not possible because he leaves so early, then leave it where he'll find it in the morning (or take it to his work) with a cute little note saying you were thinking of him and you hope he has a great day.

YOUR THOUGHTS

DAY 9

MAKE EYE CONTACT AND OFFER WORDS OF AFFIRMATION

Death and life are in the power
of the tongue, and those who
love it will eat its fruits.

—PROVERBS 18:21

Words are powerful. They can build up or tear down. Words can destroy a relationship or make it flourish. Jeff is so good about telling me every day that he loves me and is thankful for me. He is constantly telling me that I'm beautiful and that I'm a wonderful wife and mom. Can I be honest with you? Most of the time, especially lately, I sure don't feel beautiful. I probably already botched up being a wonderful wife and mom with a comment I made or by being impatient or selfish.

But when Jeff *looks me in the eyes* and speaks those words over me, I start to believe them instead of the lies I can so easily believe about myself. And that gives me life. It gives me hope. It helps me to see myself the way God sees me, and it helps me to be a better wife and mom. Insecurities fly out the door. Feelings of being overwhelmed or anxious are exchanged for courage to do the task God's given me.

It can be easy to not speak life into our men because we're too busy, but man, is it important!

LOVE IN ACTION

— Today, look your man in the eyes, tell him how thankful you are for him, and name at least one thing that you love about him.

— Think of something specific like, "I love how you provide for our family" or "I love how you listen to people and make them feel heard."

YOUR THOUGHTS

LIST 10 THINGS YOU LOVE ABOUT HIM

—

Some time ago I was praying for Jeff and asking the Lord to show me how I could encourage him that day. It had been only a week since I had given birth to our son Kannon, so I felt pretty tapped out and not able to do much for Jeff. I noticed our dry-erase marker in a basket in the bathroom. (You never know when you might need to write a little note on your bathroom mirror!)

I grabbed that bad boy and wrote out on the mirror ten things I love about Jeff. It took me probably five minutes. It wasn't pretty or designed or super well thought out. It was just a little overflow of my heart letting him know that I love him, see him, and am thankful for all he does. Later that day he told me how much that list meant to him. It totally made his day!

LOVE IN ACTION

- Today, write out ten things that you love and appreciate about your man.
- Write them on his bathroom mirror, in a note, or send them in a text.

YOUR THOUGHTS

TELL HIM HOW
HE'S GROWN

—

Let no corrupting talk come out of
your mouths, but only such as is good
for building up, as fits the occasion.

—EPHESIANS 4:29

L ife can be discouraging at times and we can get bogged
down by thinking of all the things we aren't doing right,
what we need to do differently, what we need to change, or
how we failed in a particular task. I think, too, often it's
harder to see what God is doing in us or the ways we've
grown. But God is always at work in our lives and we are
always growing if we're seeking Him.

When you're doing life with someone, it's so important
to point out areas you see them growing in because often

they don't see it themselves. There is nothing like hearing someone, especially someone close to you, tell you that you're doing an awesome job or how you've become more patient, gentle, or kind. It's so encouraging and gives you hope that you are growing, even though you're not perfect and still have room to change.

LOVE IN ACTION

- Today, tell your man at least one area that you've seen him grow in lately and how proud you are of him.
- If you're not sure what that is, spend some time praying and thinking about the past couple of weeks. When you spend time praying for your man, you will be more attuned to what God is doing in his life.
- Note: When you tell him how he's grown today, don't tell him how bad at something he used to be! Just mention how you've seen him be a certain way lately and how proud you are of him. For instance, "Babe, I've seen you be really patient with your clients this week and I'm so proud of you." Or "Thank you for taking out the trash this week without my even having to ask you."

YOUR THOUGHTS

PERFORM ONE OF HIS RESPONSIBILITIES

Bear one another's burdens, and
so fulfill the law of Christ.

—GALATIANS 6:2

I remember that after Jeff and I got married, we argued over making the bed for like the first two years! I love a made bed. It's my jam. When I'm getting things done, it's the first thing I do. I feel frazzled if it's unmade and I hate looking into our room if the bed is all messy. I'm totally okay leaving it unmade if we're running late somewhere, but otherwise I like it nice and neat.

Jeff, on the other hand, thought it was a waste of time because we're just going to sleep in it that night and get it messy again. Can anyone else relate? We went back and forth. Then, finally one day, Jeff got it. I wouldn't say he felt the same way about needing it to be made to get other things done or to feel organized, but he realized that regardless of his opinion, the fact was that making the bed was important to me and it really served me to have it made. One day I walked in, and it was made! And I'll add that he did a better job at making it than I did.

I still end up making the bed most of the time. But on those days that I walk into our room after breakfast and he's made the bed, I always stop and feel so loved in that moment. It's a small gesture, but it tells me that Jeff was thinking of me and did it to serve me.

LOVE IN ACTION

- Today, think of one of his responsibilities and do it for him. It doesn't have to be something that you guys think differently about! Think of a task that he always does that you could do for him.
- Some suggestions: take out the trash, wash his car, make his lunch for the next day, bring snacks to a meeting, etc.

YOUR THOUGHTS

_____

_____

_____

_____

_____

_____

_____

_____

_____

_____

_____

_____

_____

_____

_____

_____

_____

_____

_____

_____

_____

LET HIM KNOW YOU'RE THINKING OF HIM

—

A few years ago I had really been wanting eyelash exten-
sions, so I finally got them. Because who has time to
put on makeup with a toddler and newborn?! I told Jeff that
was my Mother's Day gift, so I wasn't expecting anything on
Mother's Day, I just wanted to be with my family and cele-
brate my mom. After we had a special breakfast and played
in the yard, both the kids fell asleep (oh, how I cherish you,
sweet nap time), so I told Jeff I was going to take a bath and
lie down for a bit.

While I was rocking Kins asleep in her room, Jeff quietly
got my bath ready. He filled it with bath salts and bubble
bath, lit a candle, put on music, grabbed my book and wrote
a little note that said "I LOVE YOU." Talk about an amazing
husband! How thoughtful was he?! You know the funny
thing though? Amid all that wonderfulness, my favorite part
was the little note that said "I LOVE YOU."

I know I'm a words person. I feel the most loved by written word. And I'll take it in any form—texts, emails, cards. But there was something just so sweet about seeing Jeff's handwriting on that bright blue card in a bold font. I still have it hanging up on my bathroom mirror.

Little surprises that say "Hey, I'm thinking of you" are always sweet and special. It's such a good feeling to know that someone has you on his or her mind. And it can be the littlest thing!

LOVE IN ACTION

- Today, put a little something in his car (or another place of your choosing) as a sweet surprise.
- It could be a little note that says "I LOVE YOU," your picture on his dashboard, or his favorite candy bar. Anything that says you're thinking of him.

YOUR THOUGHTS

POST HOW GRATEFUL YOU ARE FOR HIM

——

If you're on Facebook or Instagram, I'm sure you've seen ladies post about their men and use #MCM (Man Crush Monday). Although I always forget to post about Jeff on Mondays just like I always forget to do a #TBT (Throw Back Thursday) until Friday, I love this concept!

I think it's so great to tell others how thankful we are for our men, especially in a culture where women put down their men so often. Let's be women who speak kindly about our men, who honor them, respect them, and cheer them on.

LOVE IN ACTION

- Today, post a Facebook or Instagram message about how thankful you are for your man.
- Use #31creativeways so we can all see it and cheer one another on as women who honor their men!

YOUR THOUGHTS

REMIND HIM OF HOW YOUR STORY BEGAN

O ne of my favorite questions to ask a couple is how they met or when they knew they wanted to spend the rest of their lives together. The best is hearing the couple go back and forth, playing off each other, and hearing them recount their story.

As they talk, you can still see the sparkle in their eyes and, by the end of the story, it's apparent they are closer in some way. They are enjoying each other more than when they began because they're reminded of how sweet their story is and how much they love each other.

LOVE IN ACTION

- Bring a little sparkle back today by writing a note to your guy telling him your meeting story and when you started to fall for him.
- It can be a long letter or just a simple note to remind him of your beginnings.

YOUR THOUGHTS

ENCOURAGE
HIS DREAMS

—

Encourage one another and
build one another up.

—I THESSALONIANS 5:11

J eff and I do a journal together in which we ask each
other the same six specific questions every week (well,
we're trying to do it every week). It's a game changer. Truly.
Talking about these questions each week helps us get on the
same page and brings a lot more grace and support into our
marriage. It gives us a focus for the week and a short-term
vision for our relationship.

One of the questions we ask each other is, "What dreams
or thoughts have been on your mind this week?" Now, my
husband and I are both dreamers, so this question isn't too

difficult for us. However, Jeff is an extreme visionary, so every week he has a new dream to share! Which at times can be hard for this anxious little heart of mine. Always something new. Always something changing. Always something in the works.

The longer I'm married to Jeff, though, I'm realizing how important it is to really listen to his dreams and to encourage him in them. Even if it sounds crazy or totally 100 percent out of my comfort zone. I can share my questions, of course, but I need to cheer him on in it and dream with him first. When I do that, it's like he's a new man, fearless and able to conquer anything. But when I let my anxious heart get in the way and give him looks like, "Oh boy, another dream . . ." it completely crushes him.

I realize that Jeff is an extreme case of a dreamer and most likely your man doesn't always have a new thing on the horizon. However, all of us have dreams and all of us have thoughts throughout the week of something we're hoping to do, to accomplish, to change. For instance, in this season of my life, I don't have a lot of big dreams that I'm thinking of. However, I want to have a certain couple over for dinner next week, I want to take Kinsley to the strawberry farm next weekend, and I really want to join a barre class to tone up a bit. Thoughts. Dreams.

LOVE IN ACTION

- Today, ask your man a thought or dream that he's been chewing on this week. Something he can't stop thinking about or something that keeps coming back to his mind.
- Listen as he shares, and dream with him. Encourage him in a certain endeavor or pray over it for him.

YOUR THOUGHTS

SEND HIM A CANDY GRAM

—

When Jeff and I first started dating, it was long distance. He was in Oregon going to college and I was across the Pacific Ocean in Hawaii doing an internship at a church. Long distance definitely has it pitfalls—like you're not together! But one good thing is, it forces you to be creative. Like really creative. I mean, when you can't hang out, go on dates, or see each other at church, you're forced to find ways to show each other that you care other than through phone conversations.

One Valentine's Day I decided to make Jeff a candy gram. I went to the store and bought as many different candy bars as I could find. Then I put a bunch of construction paper together like a book and wrote him a love letter using the candy bars as fill-in words. Next thing I know, I'm getting a telephone call with Jeff on the other end, munching on a candy bar, proclaiming how awesome my candy gram was! *He loved it.*

Now, even if your man is super healthy or doesn't really do candy, I guarantee he'll love the candy gram because it's so thoughtful and creative.

LOVE IN ACTION

- Visit the grocery store or gas station and pick up some candy bars to make your own candy gram for your man.
- Some candies that work well are Symphony, 100 Grand, Milky Way, Hot Tamales, and Big Hunk.
- Make your message as short or as long as you like. You don't have to be a poet to do it! Just be creative and have fun.

YOUR THOUGHTS

PLAN A
SPECIAL DATE

———

J eff will tell you that one of his all-time favorite dates that I took him on happened when he came to Maui to visit me. My youth pastor let me borrow his truck for the night, so I couldn't wait to take Jeff out somewhere. However, being an intern, I had no money. Like zilch. So I packed a special picnic dinner for us. You know, PB&J sandwiches, apples, and cookies. I filled two Nalgene bottles with water and added some Crystal Light peach iced tea packets because I knew how much Jeff loved peach flavoring.

We drove down a little ways and then parked where we could back up to the beach. We climbed in the back of the truck, put down a blanket, and ate our picnic dinner as we watched the sun sink into the ocean. We talked, laughed, and had the best time!

LOVE IN ACTION

- Plan a special date with your guy this week. It doesn't have to be elaborate or expensive, just something that is intentional and brings you together. Think of something that he would love to do.
- If you need to get a babysitter, do it, or you can always do something when the kids go to bed. It doesn't even have to be the whole evening. You'll be surprised at how much you can pack into even an hour when you're both being intentional with each other.
- Some ideas are: have a bonfire, play a board game, chat over a fruit-and-cheese platter.

YOUR THOUGHTS

_____

_____

_____

_____

_____

_____

_____

_____

_____

_____

_____

_____

_____

_____

_____

_____

_____

_____

_____

SHARE A SPECIAL
PLACE

—

We all have our favorite places to hang out. They become "our places." Maybe you have a favorite coffee shop, a store that is always your first choice to shop, or a park where you love to go to read. For me, there's a walk down the road a bit that is right on the ocean. It's gorgeous, truly breathtaking. It's about one-and-a-half miles long and borders all the resorts on the water. It curves and has hills and is lined with tropical greenery. As you walk you can see all the boats and ships go sailing by. Some days you can spot whales far out in the ocean or turtles swimming by the shore. It's my all-time favorite place in the whole world. I've spent countless hours walking that path praying, dreaming, processing, and having heart-to-hearts with friends.

Jeff has never been someone to go for walks. He likes working out but not if it *feels* like working out! Give him basketball, paddleboarding, or swimming—anything that's fun and action-packed. But recently he's been up for walking with me. I used to have to beg him to come with me, but now if I mention I'm going on a walk, half the time he jumps at the chance to go with me! And I can't tell you how much it means to me. I love having that intentional time with him, and I love the fact that he's wanting to join me in something I love doing. So, when he goes with me on my favorite walk, it's like he's shouting from the rooftops, "I LOVE YOU, ALYSSA!"

LOVE IN ACTION

- Think of one of your man's favorite spots to hang out and go with him this week.
- If it's CrossFit or his gym, watch him or buy a one-day pass to work out together.
- If it's a music store, go and take a look at the instruments together.
- If it's a food truck, get lunch together.

YOUR THOUGHTS

"OH, HEY, HANDSOME!"

A joyful heart is good medicine.

—PROVERBS 17:22

L aughing is one of my favorite things. Tell me a good joke and it'll make my whole day. When I was in junior high, a friend and I sent each other pickup lines from a particular website. We got the biggest kick out of the ones people came up with, and bonus—the website had a new pickup line every day. I always wanted a guy to use one of the lines on me. I mean, how could a girl say no to: "Looks like you dropped something—my jaw!"

LOVE IN ACTION

- Today, find a good pickup line and use it on your guy. Text it, email it, write it in a note.
- Maybe even have a different line for him every hour!
- Whatever you do, show him you like him while giving him a good laugh.

YOUR THOUGHTS

_____

_____

_____

_____

_____

_____

_____

_____

_____

_____

_____

_____

_____

_____

_____

_____

_____

_____

_____

_____

_____

_____

_____

LET HIM PICK
THE MOVIE

———

Love does not insist on its own way.

—1 CORINTHIANS 13:5

Jeff and I love our movie nights. We don't get to the movie theater much these days, but one of our favorite things to do is pick a good movie on Netflix or Amazon Prime and cuddle up on the couch together. Jeff makes this crazy-good popcorn that we put in our special white popcorn bowls, and Aslan, our dog, sits by my feet drooling the whole time I chomp away.

As I am writing this, I'm realizing that for the most part, we always watch a movie that I want to watch. Now, don't get me wrong. Jeff will agree to the movie and want to watch it, too, but it's never one on the top of his list. He always goes ahead with one that I really want to see because he's so sweet and because I'm a lot more picky as a movie watcher. I mean, I just really love my rom-coms (romantic comedies)!

LOVE IN ACTION

- This week, watch a movie with your man but let him choose the movie.
- Pop some popcorn, get some candy, and cuddle up together.

YOUR THOUGHTS

PRACTICE THE ART OF THANK YOU

—

One key to a successful relationship is found in the two words *thank you*. Showing that you notice what he's doing and are grateful is monumental. It's a sign that you see him and appreciate him. Sometimes it can be easy to get caught up in all the things that he's not doing or ways you wish he would change, and that can be toxic.

When Jeff says thank you to me for doing the things that I normally do every day, it makes me want to keep serving him and gives me joy in the midst of it. Sometimes he'll stop me from what I'm doing, look me in the eyes, and thank me for something specific. It makes me break out in the biggest smile. It's the best!

LOVE IN ACTION

- This week, focus on saying thank you for the big and little things that your man does. For example: taking out the trash, clearing your plate, opening your door, or making you coffee.
- Today specifically, think of one thing he's done for you, look him in the eye, and say thank you.

YOUR THOUGHTS

DRAW HIM A PICTURE

—

S ince Kinsley's favorite thing in the whole world is swimming, on her second birthday we bought her an inflatable pool complete with a slide and water-ball activities. We had a little pool party with a few of her closest friends. She had a blast! She giggled and smiled the whole morning. Her friends each brought her a little gift, including a home-made card. Her friend Ace drew her a stick picture of the two of them together and handed it to her as soon as he saw her. She looked at it, pointed to each stick figure, and got the biggest smile on her face.

Cards can sometimes be the best gifts. I love how little kids draw pictures for people. I have a handful hanging up on my refrigerator right now, displayed as true pieces of artwork.

This may sound silly, but draw a picture for your man today. If you're an incredible artist, then draw something amazing! But if you're like me and stick figures are about as good as it gets, that's okay too! Really, this day's action is all about bringing the childlike wonder back into your relationship. It's just something fun and thoughtful.

LOVE IN ACTION

- Draw a picture on a sticky note or construction paper.
- Draw a picture of your man and point out his characteristics that you love.
- Or draw a picture of the two of you together.
- Maybe draw a picture of when you met, your favorite date, or one of your favorite memories.
- Or draw a picture of something you'd like to do together one day. Whatever it is, I'm sure he'll cherish it the same way Kinsley cherished her homemade birthday cards.

YOUR THOUGHTS

BE HIS CHEERLEADER

I hosted a mom's gathering this last spring with a handful of women I really wanted to get to know better. Each week they'd come over for a time of fellowship and learning. An older mom would come and share about what she has learned as a mom or wife and what God has taught her over the years. Not only did our group become tight-knit, we also were encouraged by the older women and shaped by their wisdom.

One of the ladies who came to teach shared about loving and enjoying her husband. She told us that we as wives are called to be our husbands' biggest cheerleaders. We are to stand by their sides, support them, listen well, pray diligently, and encourage them.

I had known to support and encourage Jeff but I had never heard it phrased quite that way before: be their biggest cheerleader. I love that it gives me an awesome mental picture of one of my main roles as a wife. Even if you're just dating, being a cheerleader for your man is important! Our guys need to know we believe in them and are rooting for them.

LOVE IN ACTION

- Take a picture of yourself today, holding up a sign that says "GO _____ (fill in your man's name)!"
- Send it to him sometime today, letting him know that you are cheering him on!

YOUR THOUGHTS

CREATE A BUCKET LIST

———

W e have some friends who pretty much rock at life. They're some of my favorite people ever and a couple that I really look up to. A few years ago their church focused on loving and pursuing your spouse and encouraged the couples in their congregation to go on a date with each other every week. They called it 52 in 15 (2015). As in, fifty-two dates in fifty-two weeks. At the end of the year, the couples who actually went on fifty-two dates were entered into a contest to win a weeklong vacation cruise.

That was an awesome concept! The whole purpose behind it was to encourage married couples to invest in their marriages.

This year, our friends are doing it again, but for their dates they made a bucket list; a list of fifty-two dates they want to go on with each other. It's been so fun to follow them on Instagram and see the fun dates they take. They've made a fruit pizza together, gone on a picnic, and made playlists for each other.

LOVE IN ACTION

- Sit down with your guy today or sometime this week and make a bucket list of dates you want to go on together.
- You don't need to do fifty-two! But get at least ten ideas written down.
- Make writing your bucket list a little date in itself! Get some yummy snacks, a good drink, and have fun scheming together.

YOUR THOUGHTS

USE WORDS TO TELL HIM HOW SPECIAL HE IS

—

Pleasant words are a honeycomb, sweet
to the soul and healing to the bones.

—PROVERBS 16:24

Have you ever had someone give you a card or send you a random text that tells you how special you are and even has a little list of character traits you possess that they love and admire? It's the absolute best. And if you're like me, it usually seems to come at just the moment you need it.

While I was growing up, my parents and friends would give me little notes with sweet sayings, but the one I remember most was an unexpected card from one of my close friends and mentors when I was interning at the church. It had been a long, hard day and to be honest, I was in an intense season of growth. Which is a nice way of saying I was a hot mess! The Lord was stretching me and growing me in ways I'd never imagined were possible. I walked into our office and there on my computer was an envelope with my name beautifully written on the top of it. I opened it and there was a list of things she saw in me that were beautiful. Tears stung my eyes because amid all my mess, there was a deep beauty that God was creating and continuing to perfect in me.

LOVE IN ACTION

- Words can make all the difference in someone's day.
- Send a little text to your man today with at least five genuine things that you love about him.

YOUR THOUGHTS

ASK HOW YOU CAN HELP

——

Two are better than one.

—ECCLESIASTES 4:9

This past year, Jeff has started to ask me, before the day starts or after a heart-to-heart, what he can do to help me that day. How can he serve me? And each time he asks me, my heart softens and calms. Sometimes, I do have some things for him to do that would really be helpful to me. But for the most part, it brings me peace and encouragement that he just asks. It shows me that he's thinking of me and reminds me that we're a team. I'm not alone. I don't have to do everything on my own because he's there to help me. Which, for me, is so encouraging because I tend to get overwhelmed easily.

LOVE IN ACTION

- Ask your guy if there's anything you can do to help him today.
- Is there any way you can serve him?
- Be prepared if he does have something for you to do and do it cheerfully! But know that just asking will encourage him too.

YOUR THOUGHTS

PRESENT HIM WITH APPRECIATION ABCS

—

Today's suggestion will take a little more time and thought than some of the others, but I promise you it will be something that will really bless and honor him.

Pinterest is full of cute little ways to show your man you love him. One year for Valentine's Day, I rummaged through a whole list of DIY ideas of things I could make for Jeff. I noticed a deck of cards strung together with holes punched through the tops. On each card, they had written a characteristic trait that they loved about their man. It was so cute! I whipped one up (well, not quite that easy!) for Jeff. I remember seeing the look on his face when he opened it and read each card. He was so touched that I had spent so much time coming up with fifty-two things that I love about him. It's still on his side table by the bed as a little reminder that I love him so.

LOVE IN ACTION

- For today, I won't ask you to come up with fifty-two things you love about your man! However, twenty-six things seems pretty doable. Get twenty-six little cards together, twenty-six sticky notes, or just a sheet of paper and write out the ABCs.
- For each letter of the alphabet, come up with a character trait or something your man does that you love for each letter of the alphabet. It doesn't have to be poetic or artsy. Just dot down twenty-six things you love about him.

YOUR THOUGHTS

_____

_____

_____

_____

_____

_____

_____

_____

_____

_____

_____

_____

_____

_____

_____

_____

_____

_____

_____

_____

_____

_____

TAKE HIM HIS FAVORITE DRINK

———

When Jeff and I first started dating, I thought one of the ways a guy shows you he loves you and is pursuing you is by bringing you your favorite drink from time to time. In all fairness I did grow up in Seattle, home of the coffee bean. (Okay, it's totally not the home of the coffee bean, but man do we love our coffee!) So I frequented coffee shops. And if you know me, you know that one of the ways to my heart is coffee. Straight up, just bring me a cup of coffee with a heavy dose of creamer and I'll love you forever.

Jeff never brought me coffee when we were first dating because of the geographical distance between us. The few times we were actually together, he just didn't know that fact about me because, again, long distance. You just don't know those day-in and day-out things about the other person when you're never around them. If I'm honest with you, I'll say that this did factor into my breaking up with Jeff the first time. I didn't think he liked me that much. It's a long story,

87

but man, was I wrong. Wrong about Jeff not liking me and wrong that true love was summed up in a coffee drink!

I know now true love is about so much more than providing favorite drinks. It's more about faithfulness, kindness, forgiveness, and grace. However, knowing the little ways that show your person you like them and know them is important, and, for me, that's coffee. Jeff knows that about me now and will bring me special drinks from time to time. I still remember our second year of marriage, he came home one day with two Starbucks red cups—the first of the season! Talk about *true love*!

LOVE IN ACTION

- Today, get your man his favorite drink.
- Maybe it's coffee or maybe it's a soda, kombucha, or a special water.
- Take it to him at work, school, or have it waiting for him at home. He'll love the kind gesture.

YOUR THOUGHTS

BUY HIM A GIFT

—

I'm not gonna lie. I love getting gifts! Not just any gifts but ones that are super thoughtful and so me. When I open a gift from someone and it's exactly what I like, my heart is completely melted because I feel known and loved. It doesn't have to be anything big or expensive. (I mean, this girl does love her diamonds, but really . . .) It can be the smallest thing—and honestly, sometimes that's even better—like chocolate in a mason jar because those two things are my love language.

One time I mentioned to my mom how much I love flowers and that I decided every time I go grocery shopping, I'm going to buy a little bouquet of flowers as a treat to myself. Even if it's just one sunflower, it brings me so much joy. Since mentioning my love for flowers to my mom, she has brought me flowers every other week. Now, of course, I didn't tell my mom I loved flowers so that she would buy me flowers. But because she is the most thoughtful person in the world, she always thinks of me when she runs into the grocery store and buys me a bouquet because she knows how much they mean to me. (I know, she's the best!)

As much as I like receiving gifts, I love giving them even more. I love thinking of a gift that would bless someone I love. The best is when I'm out and about and I see something that screams the name of one of my friends or family members. I have to get it. Even if it's a "just because" gift.

LOVE IN ACTION

— A gift doesn't have to cost much at all; it can be the simplest thing, as long as it says, "I'm thinking of you." Go out today and get a little something for your man.

— Maybe it's his favorite candy bar, a pair of his favorite socks, a few guitar picks, a new book that he's been wanting, or a couple of movie tickets. Anything that says, "You are loved and known."

YOUR THOUGHTS

MAKE A "THANKFUL" LIST

Love rejoices with the truth.

—I CORINTHIANS 13:6

I t's really easy to complain and think of all the things you'd like to be different, right? Unfortunately, this is really easy to do when it comes to your man. There have been times when I let my mind wander and think of how I'd like Jeff to be different. Or, rather, things I wish he'd do differently— how he could change. Areas he needs to grow in. Things I dislike; stuff I get frustrated or irritated by. Yuck! Even just writing this out, I feel trapped and down.

It's good to recognize areas your man can grow in, to pray for him, and encourage him to be the best version of himself that he can be. But it's never good to fall into a pit of ungratefulness and complaints. It's toxic and not only will it bring you down, it will bring down the relationship.

Cultivating a heart of thankfulness is so vital in all of life, as well as in a relationship. Thinking about how thankful you are for your man and listing the ways you're thankful for him is so important.

LOVE IN ACTION

- Today's task isn't so much for your man as for you. Fostering a thankful heart for him will naturally overflow into your relationship and will affect how you see him. You'll become more joy-filled, grateful, and kind, instead of complaining, nagging, or harboring bitterness.
- Today list ways that you are thankful for your man. It can be the littlest thing to the biggest thing. Have fun remembering all the ways he is a blessing in your life!
- Find a creative way to present your list to him and keep a copy somewhere you can access easily when you need to be reminded of the positive things in your relationship.

YOUR THOUGHTS

DAY 32

YOUR TURN

———

Y ou didn't think there was going to be a Day 32, did ya? We thought we'd add one more day and turn it over to you.

LOVE IN ACTION

— Think of an idea, a gesture—any kind thing you can do for your significant other today.
— Be creative. Be loving. And most of all, show him how much you care.
— Also, we'd love to hear what you picked for Day 32! We might even end up including it in future versions or volumes of this book.
— Upload your idea at upload.31creativeways.com. We can't wait to hear how creative you guys are and what y'all came up with!

YOUR THOUGHTS

_____

_____

_____

_____

_____

_____

_____

_____

_____

_____

_____

_____

_____

_____

_____

_____

_____

_____

_____

_____

AFTERWORD

First off, you all rock! For reals. Complete rock stars. Why? Because you care about your relationship. You're investing in it. You believe in it. It matters to you.

We believe that a relationship is like a garden. For it to flourish it needs proper nourishment, constant care, awareness of the things trying to hurt it, and sometimes it gets a little messy. This book is just a start to hopefully continuing or taking that leap of putting you and your significant other on the path to a vibrant and beautiful relationship.

So thank you for taking this journey with us. Thank you for reading this book. And thank you for just being you. We'd love to hear from you and how the challenge went by sharing something online with the hashtag #31creativeways. We are constantly on that hashtag to see all the awesome stuff you guys are doing and ways you tweaked one of our challenges to make it work for you.

We love when folks give us a shout on social media, so feel free to stop by and say hey!

Would love to e-meet you.

STOP BY AND SAY HI!

Instagram and Twitter:
@jeffersonbethke and @alyssajoybethke

Facebook:
fb.com/jeffersonbethkepage and fb.com/alyssajoybethke

Snapchat:
jeffersonbethke

Website:
jeffandalyssa.com

ABOUT THE
AUTHORS

Jefferson and Alyssa Bethke live in Maui with their three kids: Kinsley, Kannon, and Lucy. They write books (including *Jesus > Religion*, *It's Not What You Think*, *Love Is*, *To Hell with the Hustle*, *Take Back Your Family*, *Spoken For*, and *Satisfied*), make online videos, and host a podcast or two. Their mission is to equip and encourage people to follow Jesus in their day-to-day. They have a yellow lab named Aslan and enjoy reading good books and drinking good coffee during their downtime.

You can read more at JeffandAlyssa.com.